7 Keys to Prophetic Maturity

The Practice of the Prophetic, Volume 1

by

Sam Medina

7 Keys to Prophetic Maturity
The Practice of the Prophetic, Volume 1
Copyright © 2012 Samuel Medina

Published in Toronto by The Restoration Group
via
CreateSpace Independent Publishing Platform
ISBN 13-:978-1483997087
ISBN-10: 1483997081

Foreword

Recently, someone asked me for advice on how to further develop in their prophetic gifting. I thought about this for a while, since I have never much liked the notion that gifts from God can be 'developed,' as I see them more as being further revealed as we grow in faith and character. However, I knew what this young prophet had meant: he wanted to be able to hear from God more often, more clearly, and to be able to administer the gift more effectively.

What I've taught prophets over the years is to develop a lifestyle of prayer and fasting, and to 'exercise' spiritually through the study of and meditation upon God's word. Additionally, I have over time come to understand that there are several habits you can develop which will be conducive to maturity in the prophetic, and in other matters as well.

These habits, coupled with a basic understanding of the prophetic, are essential to the proper execution of every ministerial gift, and it is my hope that my attempt to explain them may prove to be of benefit and blessing to you as you read this book.

THE PROPHET: DISTINCTIVES AND DIRECTIVES

The prophet, and the prophetic are often greatly misunderstood in the church world. In the churches we attended while I was a child, it was commonly believed that John the Baptist was the very last of the prophets, and that therefore it was impossible for anyone in this present era to be a prophet. As I grew older, asking why the book of Acts referred to Paul, Silas, Agabus, and others as being prophets years after John had been executed was a sure recipe for trouble.

For reasons unknown, and perhaps not too mysterious, certain elements of the Spanish-speaking churches had been taught to believe something which contradicted the Bible outright, and apparently many among them had not investigated the question for themselves. In the Biblical record, there are many instances in which God's people began to fall into error.

"In those days *there was* no king in Israel: every man did *that which was* right in his own eyes." (Judges 21:25)

This final verse of the Book of Judges tells us a good deal about our own human tendency to operate according to our own perception and understanding, which are all too often misguided or just plain wrong. In the case of the churches which did not believe in the existence of contemporary prophets, it should not be too surprising that there were other serious problems which also arose from a lack of understanding of the Bible. This brings us to our point, which is the illustration of the purpose and function of the prophet.

Among the diverse purposes of the prophetic is to reveal the mind of God to His people, and to bring order and clarity into matters in which error or confusion have arisen. This is sometimes through prophetic utterances which correct, rebuke, uncover secret sins, or which simply communicate a message of repentance, hope, or encouragement. In all cases, the prophet and his message are always intended to restore God's people to unbroken fellowship with the Lord.

Who, or even what, then, is the prophet? The word 'prophet' is used more than 400 times throughout the Bible. The first use of the word occurs in Genesis 20:7.

> "Now therefore restore the man *his* wife; for he *is* a **prophet**, and he shall pray for thee, and thou shalt live: and if thou restore *her* not, know thou that thou shalt surely die, thou, and all that *are* thine."

The word used here in the Hebrew is *nabiy*, which defined as follows:

> *nabiy'* naw-bee' from 5012; a prophet or (generally) inspired man:-- prophecy, that prophesy, prophet. (05030, *Strong's Hebrew Lexicon of the Bible*)

The root for this word is *nabá (05012, Strong's)*, which signifies to speak by inspiration. In the historical context of the word, we ought to understand that such inspiration was assumed to be divine in the sense that a god or gods were moving the prophet to speak or sing. Thus we must understand, that the Biblical prophet is someone who is gifted in such a way as to operate under divine inspiration. The Biblical record is clear that some prophets did not always receive their inspiration from God. For example, in 1 Kings 22 there is a group of about 400 prophets who were given a lying spirit by God himself in order to assure the Ahab would go to his doom, and there were prophets who served other gods, as in the case of Elijah's confrontation with those who served Baal in 1 Kings 18.

We delve into the identity and definition of the prophet in more detail in *The Practice of the Prophetic: A Comprehensive Study,* but for the purposes of this book we will define the Christian prophet as one who receives inspiration and communication from God by way of an innate gift. The prophet is perhaps unique in that the office appears to be conferred in the womb, and the gift is often seen to function to some extent whether the prophet is saved or not.

> Before I formed you in the womb I knew you; Before you were born I sanctified you; I ordained you a prophet to the nations. (Jeremiah 1:5, NKJV)

We can therefore see that the prophet is ordained in the womb, before any decision to serve God has been made. It is perhaps because of this that the prophet's gift appears to be 'tuned in' even before he has come to know Christ as Lord and Savior. When I was in college and not living for God at all, I would sometimes lay my hand on a textbook and jokingly say to my roommate, "I'm learning by osmosis." I would then proceed to class and impress the professor with my understanding of material I had never even read. In one case, this understanding was so detailed that the professor commented that in eighteen years of teaching on that book, he had never realized the particular details I had brought up. To this day, I still haven't read that book. Thus from personal experience, I have known the prophetic gift to 'work' even when one is not Spirit-filled or in right standing with God. This is not to say that we ought to live in such a manner, or that the prophetic is ever to be used according to our self-will. Both are dangerous paths to tread, and which lead only to damnation. Remember that Lucifer's fall began with two words: "I will."

That being said, the prophet thus appears to be distinct from those with the gift of prophecy, who typically are only prophetic when the gift is in operation. The gift of prophecy is bestowed by the Holy Spirit after the individual has believed the Gospel and has been filled with the Holy Spirit. This does not lessen the value of people with a gift of prophecy; it only means that their purpose is different. However, in the case of both the prophet and the person gifted with prophecy, the pursuit of a close walk with God and the maturity that will result from that walk are not only beneficial, but necessary for their growth into the fullness of their purpose in His kingdom.

KEY #1: AVOID TALKING TOO MUCH

"In the **multitude of words** there wanteth not sin: but he that refraineth his lips is wise." (Proverbs 10:19)

For many of us, our mouth is our biggest problem. Throughout the world examples abound of people who could have avoided embarrassment, heartache, and even death, had they only watched their words a bit more carefully. There was in fact incident years ago in which two people were being robbed at gunpoint. One of them, who had been known for her wit and somewhat sassy disposition, said to the robber," What're you gonna do, shoot us?" The man shot them both dead. We can speculate as to whether he would have shot them anyway had she bit her tongue, but we can perhaps all agree that it wasn't the wisest thing to say, given the situation.

For those of us who wish to serve in ministry, and perhaps especially for those of us who are called to function in the prophetic, the ability of exercise discipline in what we say, how we say it, and when we say it is of paramount importance. This is not limited to "ministry" situations, but rather it is a habit to be cultivated in every aspect of our lives.

A good man out of the good treasure of the heart bringeth forth good things: and an evil man out of the evil treasure bringeth forth evil things. But I say unto you, That every idle word that men shall speak, they shall give account thereof in the day of judgment. (Matthew 12:35-6)

Consider what this implies about those of us who talk too much.

Our lack of discipline in our words stems from a lack of discipline in heart, and whatever we have in that undisciplined heart is bound to come out of our mouth, one way or another. The more we talk, the more likely we are to let the carnality or our own imperfections and character flaws take center stage. This is important not only because we will be accountable for what we say. The point of this passage is not merely to frighten us with the reality that even our idle words will be called into account, but to cause us to consider *why* they will be a matter for the day of judgment.

> Death and life are in the power of the tongue: and they that love it shall eat the fruit thereof. (Proverbs 18:21)

The words we speak, idle or not, have the power of life and death, and very often something said thoughtlessly can have long-term implications for those who heard and were influenced by it. For those of us who serve in the work of the ministry, whether in a formal capacity or not, we must also consider that the gifts we carry and function in serve to create a perception of who we are which also may in some cases lend an importance to our words that may not have been ascribed to them otherwise. In a word, your being influential, or being perceived as spiritual may very well cause your words to carry more weight than you may have intended.

About 15 years ago, the assistant pastor of the church I attended took it upon himself to give me a colorful nickname. It was not intended with any malice, but I found it genuinely annoying, and I really didn't want other people to get into the habit of calling me by that name as well. Admittedly, the main reason I was annoyed was that he had in his teaching related a story of how a student at the school where he worked had given him a sort of nickname. He had rebuked that student because it was disrespectful to call him by something other than his name. Thus, being the analytical kind of guy that I am, I couldn't help but take his nicknaming me to be a clear message to everyone that he did not respect me and was not to be respected by others. So, during this somewhat insecure period of my life, I was resolved not to let this go any further. I took him aside and explained my concerns to him, and told him, "If you want a guarantee that the people will follow your example, all you have to do is set a bad one. People might not follow the good examples, but they sure will follow the bad ones."

Looking back on this incident, I can freely admit that most of my concern was rooted in my personal pride and insecurity, but nevertheless there was some validity to what I had said to him. Because of his position in leadership, those under his authority and influence might well have interpreted things in the same way. The people you influence may not be hanging on your every word, but they may well indeed take what you say and run with it, so it's best to be sure that your words are well-chosen. Now, this doesn't mean we can't be truthful, or corrective for that matter. It does mean we ought not to be careless in how and when we speak.

Sometimes, even when we try to avoid idle and evil speaking, we still end up talking too much. Especially in today's westernized church, there is a good deal about the culture which seems to push us toward talking more than we really need to. I'm not saying that we shouldn't have conversations, friendships, and so on, but rather that sometimes we have a tendency to talk simply to have something to do. For some of us, this tendency has more to do with a certain degree of self-absorption and just loving the sound of our own voices. In any of these scenarios, the dangers presented by idle speech remain in play.

One of the dangers of idle and excessive talk, which may not always be obvious, is that we can very well end up missing something God had to tell or show us because we were too busy talking to listen or otherwise be able to perceive what God was revealing to us. Yes, God is perfectly capable of getting your attention in spite of how much of a blabbermouth you might be, but in many cases He will allow you to choose whether you will be ready to hear and understand. If you think this isn't possible, consider this:

10

For this people's heart is waxed gross, and their ears are dull of hearing, and **their eyes they have closed;** lest at any time they should see with their eyes, and hear with their ears, and should understand with their heart, and should be converted, and I should heal them. (Matthew 13:15)

Your speaking habits are an excellent indicator of where your heart is with respect to God, and the content of your conversation will reveal much about your inner life. From the above passage we can see that people can indeed 'close' their ears to hearing from God, and one of the ways they do this is through the sin which invariably arises from idle and excessive talk.

When God gives someone a prophetic message to deliver it is never his intention for us to put our own spin on it, or to 'edit' it, or to even 'spice it up,' as some have been known to do. Yes, God can use your personality, but that never suggests that any specific message from him is to be filtered through your personality. Indeed, throughout scripture, every faithful prophet delivered God's messages as instructed. Those who did otherwise met with terrible consequences indeed. The four hundred prophets who made a habit of telling Ahab what he wanted to hear ended up with a lying spirit send by God himself (1 Kings 22).

A fool uttereth all his mind: but a wise man keepeth it in till afterwards. (Proverbs 29:11)

If you always feel compelled to "speak your mind," then I regret to inform you that the Bible says you are a fool. That may seem harsh, but if it applies to you, lay aside the notion of being offended and make a decision to change your ways. Not every thought that comes to mind is a good or useful one, and even the best of our thoughts aren't always meant to be disclosed to everyone. In every area of life, developing a habit of **not** always speaking your mind can spare you from a great deal of unnecessary grief and conflict. Always remember that your words may have more influence than you intended, and that especially in the work of the ministry, the lost and the saved alike don't need to hear **you.** Yes, God may very well use your personality, your experiences, your testimony, but in the end, what a lost and sin-sick world need is God, not you or me. As brilliant as our minds might be, they are a poor substitute for Christ and Him crucified, so an essential part of coming to maturity as a believer, prophetic or not, is learning to exercise righteous discretion when speaking.

In my own experience over the years I have found that those who were the most chatty were always also those who had the least to offer spiritually. Some of them were even genuinely gifted, but rarely had a real word from God because their love of their own voice predisposed them to spending very little time listening to God or anyone else. The Book of Proverbs tells us that even a fool is counted wise when he holds his peace (Proverbs 17:28) and in Ecclesiastes were are told that the voice of a fool is known by the multitude of words (Ecclesiastes 5:3).

Yes, there may be times when God will give you a lot to say. However, there's a big difference between God giving you a definite message and just talking for its own sake. My challenge to you in this matter is to begin taking a thorough inventory of your habits of speech, and to develop discipline in everything you say.

A Prayer for Discipline in Speech

Father, forgive me for every idle, unnecessary, unkind, and evil word I have spoken. Cleanse my mind and mouth, and purify my thoughts that my words may bring light and life into every place I go. Teach me to bridle my tongue, and grant me wisdom to speak with your purpose and presence, in Jesus' name.

Putting it into action:

1. Spend less time talking about problems and more time praying about them and dealing with them.
2. Be purposeful in your conversations. More to the point, be kingdom-minded when you speak. This doesn't mean you have to have your head in the clouds. Just start making a habit of putting God first every time you do open your mouth.
3. Avoid gossip. The Bible condemns it repeatedly (Lev. 19;16,

Prov. 11:13, 18:8, .e.g). It can easily contaminate your walk with God, as well as impair your ability to hear clearly from God. When others try to gossip around you, steer the conversation in a better direction. If they persist, politely tell them that you have no interest in such conversation because it is ungodly. Walk away if you must. In some cases the other individuals will respect your integrity and might even correct their own ways, and in other instances you may very well lose some friends. In either case, always remember that the integrity of your priesthood is far more important than the favor of men.

KEY #2: MASTER THE ART OF WATCHFUL SILENCE

Hear counsel, and receive instruction, that you may be wise in your latter end. (Proverbs 19:20)

How can we hear counsel if were's too busy talking? Or how can we receive instruction if we're not really paying attention? One habit which I've found to be absolutely necessary for maturity in the prophetic is that of what I like to call watchful silence. This is more than just getting quiet, and more than meditation. It is a matter of making it your lifestyle to be always ready to hear from God. Sometimes we can convince ourselves that we're already in a good position to hear from God, while the truth is that our mind is so cluttered with our own opinions, the opinions of others, and the general spiritual 'noise' of culture that even when we do hear, it isn't very clear. Before we can really understand how to achieve that watchful silence, we have to deal with all the noise that's kept us from our purpose.

Thou preparest a table before me in the presence of mine enemies: thou anointest my head with oil; my cup runneth over. (Psalm 23:5)

The table is set, but are you eating? A lot of times God has placed so much around us to spiritually feed us and to teach us, but we fail to notice it because we're too occupied with our own ideas, agendas and desires. When I was in college, I once got so caught up in a game I was playing that I lost track of time, and then ran to the dining hall, thinking I was about to miss dinner. To make a long story short, I had missed dinner, breakfast and lunch, and had nearly missed dinner again. Spiritually, many of us have a tendency to do the same thing. Sometimes it's with our woes and troubles, and sometimes its the various good times of life and ministry that get us so caught up in the work of the Lord that we forget the Lord of the work. There's a variety of ways in which this happens to us.

Simply being busy is among them, as we've mentioned above, so we need not go into further detail in regard to those factors. Another significant factor is in our submission. The above verse from Psalm 23 makes reference to the ancient practice of smearing the heads of sheep with oil to protect them from flies and other parasites which could torment the sheep not just with their bites, but also by laying their eggs in the sheep's noses and ears. The subsequent irritation and infection could lead to the sheep being unable to smell predators, as well being unable to eat. In some cases, the sheep's ears could become infected as well, and then they could have difficulty in hearing their shepherd's voice. Untreated, sheep can easily die from such infections. The oil also protected the sheep from other parasites which could spread quickly among the flock, since sheep greet one another by rubbing their heads together.

However, it would be difficult indeed to thoroughly anoint a sheep who is struggling, kicking or biting, and very often that's just what we do in our relationship with God through our self-will and in relationships with earthly authorities God has placed in our lives. The result is that we become susceptible to the 'noise' and 'infection' of the cares of this world, the devices of the enemy, and the various lusts of the flesh. As a result, rather than being a blessing, we become a danger to the flock. It is best then that we examine ourselves and repent of rebellion, stubbornness and self-will so that we are not hindered in being able to hear from God.

Once we start dealing with those issues, then we're in a better position to learn to be truly quiet in our spirit. When rebellion and distractions are out o the way, you'll find it easier to be ready to hear from the Lord. Now, this is not to be mistaken for **trying** to hear from God. Nowhere in the Bible will you ever find an account of a prophet who had to **try** to hear from God. God spoke, the prophet listened, and that was it. Watchful silence is more of a habit of simply being available and ready to listen, while remaining alert and attentive.

The study of the Bible is vital to developing this kind of stillness. More than the mere habit of reading scripture out of a sense of obligation, to prepare a sermon, or to research for some purpose or other, it will greatly benefit you to read the word just for its own sake. Relax, sit down, and enjoy the word of God in all its beauty and wisdom.

Another good exercise for developing this habit is to practice conversation with others in which you carefully consider their words without focusing on what you are going to say next. Indeed, in the ordinary conversations of this mortal life, many misunderstandings occur simply because we were working so hard at thinking of what to say that we were not listening well enough to rightly understand what the other person was saying.

Many of us take this pattern of self-centered behavior into our relationship with God. We can be so focused on what we want, what our problems are, and everything we feel we need to say to God that we either aren't listening at all, or we're not listening as attentively as we could. In yet other cases we listen attentively, but our perception is muddled and prejudiced by our own preconceived notions, opinions, and ideologies, some of which are misguided, ill-conceived, or even the result of ungodly soul ties with the cultures we come from.

A Prayer for Quietness of Spirit

Father, please forgive me for all the ways in which my self-will and self-centeredness have kept me from hearing you clearly, and give me a heart that is able and willing to listen when you speak, in Jesus' name.

16

Putting it into action:

1. Set aside some genuine quiet time for the reading of the Word of God daily. During this time, just read it for its own sake, and do not talk. Read slowly, carefully, and thoughtfully.

2. Practice listening without focusing on what you will say next. Listen more attentively, and consider what people are **not** saying as well as what they **are** saying. As time goes on, you will learn a great deal more about people, and in many cases you will find that God has spoken to you through people more often than you may have suspected.

3. Train yourself to be more observant. A good way to do this is to take a photo, look at it for a few minutes then turn it over and write down everything you remember. Begin to be more watchful around people and the places you go, as well. As you do this, you will find that you will notice a good many more things than you did before, and you will inevitably become better able to notice when God chooses to speak through quiet things, or through the little details that we often ignore.

KEY #3: WORSHIP AND PRAYER WITHOUT AN AGENDA

God is a Spirit: and they that worship him must worship him in spirit and in truth. (John 4:24)

Most of us will make the claim of being true worshippers, and some of us certainly are. However, it's high time that we own up to the fact that while we may be true worshippers, we don't always worship in truth. Before anyone gets offended at reading this statement, I'll be the first to confess that I know what it is to be 'worshipping,' all the while I really just want something from God and I'm hoping He'll let me have my way. I'm not saying that it's wrong to have needs or to make requests of God, but all too often we approach Him in 'worship' **because** we want something.

An honest look at such a habit in our worship life would reveal that it's not the most sincere worship at best, and at worst it's an attempt at manipulation. While it's **impossible** to manipulate an omniscient God who already knows what we're up to, most of us have at least to some extent been guilty of trying to butter God up so that we can get what we want. For some of us, this sort of behavior can be attributed to the relationship habits we developed as children when we'd lavish affection on a parent in the hope of getting our way. I have some news for you, God is your Father, but He's not your sugar daddy, and He sure isn't going to fall for the same old tricks you used on your earthly parents as a child.

Some of us took this behavior well into our adulthood, and many of our relationships are corrupted and even poisoned by it. If we are going to come to a place of maturity and godly fruitfulness in the prophetic, we are going to have to turn away from these unfortunate tendencies of our Adamic nature. For many of us, this problem has been compounded by the way in which contemporary ministry often teaches that "what you can't obtain in the natural you can worship into your life."

It is not wrong to pray for specific things, including needs and desires. However, worship was never intended to be a means of getting what you want. The worship of God is, in fact, the rightful response to being aware of his existence. In a word, God is to be worshipped simply because He is God.

He came unto his own, and his own received him not. But as many as received him, to them gave he power to become the sons of God, *even* to them that believe on his name: Which were born, not of blood, nor of the will of the flesh, nor of the will of man, but of God. (John 1:11-13)

Consider this for a moment. God, in his mercy, provided a means whereby our sin could be forgiven and through which our otherwise meaningless and wasted life could be not merely redeemed, but exalted to the status of a Son of God. This not not meant only in the mere sense of adoption as sons as we understand the term. We must for a moment set aside our Western thinking and consider the context within this passage was written.

At the time the Gospel of John was written, most of the New Testament had not yet been written and compiled. Nor would it have been widely distributed. Thus, the "scriptures" known to the Church at that time would have been what we now regard as the Old Testament. It is from those books of the Bible that the early apostles taught, and from which the early Church acquired their understanding of God, Christ, and the Kingdom. This is of utmost importance to understanding our status as 'the Sons of God.' To a believer of the early New Testament era, the phrase 'Sons of God,' had a profound implication, including not only that of offspring as we know it, but also that of those higher beings identified throughout the Old Testament writings as the *b'nai elohim*, the Sons of God, more than the mere walking handful of dirt that our fallen state reduced us to. Is not such an elevation, granted by grace through faith, and so utterly underserved, reason enough for the saved man to worship God? Is our restoration to kinship with the Creator of the universe not enough to warrant our wholehearted adoration? We must remember that His blessing is the inevitable result of faithful service to Him, but not the reason for that service.

Thou shalt not bow down to their gods, nor serve them, nor do after their works: but thou shalt utterly overthrow them, and quite break down their images.
And ye shall serve the Lord your God, and he shall bless thy bread, and thy water; and I will take sickness away from the midst of thee. (Exodus 23:24-25)

Coming to (and, indeed remaining) in that place of genuine worship without pretense or ulterior motives requires us also to forsake the gods set before us by the world. In the ancient world (and to some extent today) these were obvious idols of stone and wood and metal. However, for many of us, newer, more insidious gods have arisen through culture, and thereby so much of our worship has become contaminated. If we are indeed to worship in spirit and in truth, we must also begin to evaluate those aspects of our cultures which are in conflict with the principles and truth of God's kingdom.

In the case of culture, much of this contamination is accomplished through cultural icons, which can include institutions, historical figures, celebrities, and ideologies. For every believer, including those of us functioning in the prophetic, we must be willing to turn away from anything and everything which contradicts God's word.

Out of the same mouth proceedeth blessing and cursing. My brethren, these things ought not so to be. Doth a fountain send forth at the same place sweet *water* and bitter? (James 3:10-11)
Can our worship be in truth if our words, thoughts and deeds

are indicative of admiration of or agreement with anything or anyone which is clearly against the truth of God and His word?

Some will speak of grace and mercy on this point, but we must understand that God is merciful and gracious, the grace of God is never a license to persist in willful ungodliness. If we are in pursuit of maturity, then we must in earnest pursue a purity of consecration and devotion unfettered by all those things we have clung to because of the inordinate affection we bestowed upon them through habit and culture.

Once we recognize this, we can proceed to a more deeper worship, a kind of devotion that seeks only a closer walk, and a more intimate fellowship. Yes, there are times when we must be specific in prayer and when supplication and requests are to be made. There is also, however, a wondrous place of relationship in which we pray and worship in the spirit without 'wanting' anything other than to connect with God. I have found that some of the most detailed and profound prophetic revelations and insights God gave me came while worshipping in this manner, and I am persuaded that such fellowship is essential not only for our service in the prophetic, but also for the health of our relationship with God.

A Prayer for a new place of worship in truth

Father, please forgive me for every time I've worshipped with my heart not right, whether because of personal agendas or wrongful perceptions. Give me a heart for a pure worship, a heart to seek you in truth, in Jesus' name.

Putting it into action:

1. Set aside time to simply worship God, not only at a 'special' time of day, but even throughout the day. Even as the Psalm 34:1 declares, "I will bless the Lord at all times, and his praise shall continually be in my mouth," begin to find ways to make time to adore your God, even if it's just a moment or two here and there during your day. Let His praise become part of all of your life.

2. Take some time to pray in the spirit, without any agenda,

desires, requests, etc. Sing in the spirit, let the Holy Spirit use you, and let Him sort out the details. Let that be your time just just shower God with your adoration, and to allow Him to move in you.

KEY #5: DISCRETION

Discretion shall preserve thee, understanding shall keep thee: to deliver thee from the way of the evil *man*, from the man that speaketh froward things; who leave the paths of uprightness, to walk in the ways of darkness; who rejoice to do evil, *and* delight in the frowardness of the wicked; whose ways *are* crooked, and *they* froward in their paths: to deliver thee from the strange woman, *even* from the stranger *which* flattereth with her words; which forsaketh the guide of her youth, and forgetteth the covenant of her God. For her house inclineth unto death, and her paths unto the dead. None that go unto her return again, neither take they hold of the paths of life. That thou mayest walk in the way of good *men*, and keep the paths of the righteous. For the upright shall dwell in the land, and the perfect shall remain in it. But the wicked shall be cut off from the earth, and the transgressors shall be rooted out of it. (Proverbs 2:11-22)

This passage from the Book of Proverbs makes is very clear that discretion is among the essentials of life for those who would live righteously, and so it is also essential for anyone who desires to function in the fullness of the prophetic gifting God has placed in them.

How you conduct yourself in all matters, prophetic and otherwise, will in many ways determine the extent to which you will live out the calling on your life, and few things can hinder someone's purpose like unwise decisions and behavior. Let us look at the example of David. Some theologians believe that he was conceived through his father's indiscretion, and that this was the reason why he was left tending the sheep when the prophet asked for all the sons to be present because one would be anointed to be King of Israel. Now, that theory may be correct, and it may not be, but the fact remains that while it was 'promotion time' in the house of Jesse, David was left out of the loop. Yes, the prophet ended up insisting that no one sit to dinner until the youngest son was brought forth, but what is the contemporary prophet or prophetic minister to do when the apparent season for promotion doesn't come just yet?

In some cases, we really weren't ready, in some instances the leadership just wasn't able to see as clearly as we would have liked them to, and sometimes they had some insecurity issues of their own that caused them to deliberately overlook some of the budding prophets in their midst. If this has happened or is happening to you, don't let it get to you. In fact, you ought to be encouraged, because God sure didn't miss it. When these kinds of situations occur, God is also doing a deeper work in our character.

One reality that the young prophetic minister must accept is that that leaders are people. Your pastor, bishop, etc. is just a human being. They **will** make mistakes, have problems, shortcomings, character flaws, and the like. However, you still have to work on you, and it will often occur that their imperfections, foibles, and misconduct may very well be used by God to work out your own character issues. During all this you'll need to continually forgive and let go of the little (and big) resentments that can easily defile you.

In my own experience, there were times that it seemed I'd been passed up, overlooked, underestimated and ignored, and that those in leadership were determined to never put me to any better use than cleaning the church and singing on the worship team. I'll admit it was frustrating, and it didn't help that the worship team members could be pretty nasty when they wanted to be. Though it wasn't **their** intent, in time I came to see them and their behavior as part of the process of separating me from pride and the emotionally entangling aspects of the peer-bonding dynamics of human social interaction that are often detrimental to a prophet's focus. Essentially, one of the dangers relationships pose for the prophet is that he can allow his emotional attachments to prejudice his insight. I'm not saying we can't have friends or relationships, but rather that the prophet will usually have few friends, and that he **must** learn to keep the influence his relationships from encroaching on his insight.

In those younger days I was less discreet than I am now, and on one particular day, I had just about had it with the petty behavior of some of the worship leaders. Some of their ways really got under my skin, especially since there was often sin in the camp, so to speak. In one of these instances I responded to their rotten behavior by telling them something to the effect that they ought not to be giving me a hard time when all of them were in sexual sin. I wasn't guessing, and they knew it.

It didn't take long for the pastor of the church to call me into his office, where we had a conversation I'll never forget. He agreed that I had discerned correctly concerning the other worship leaders. and then said to me, "Just because you see it, don't mean you have to say it. You don't tell everything you know." In all honesty, it was obvious that he was motivated primarily by the fact that he was trying to grow his church and didn't want anyone rocking the boat by exposing sin. However, there was some valuable truth to his words.

Whether you have the gift of prophecy or you are called to the office of the prophet, it is rarely constructive to release what you've seen or otherwise perceived spiritually simply because someone angered you. Indeed, human anger never works the righteousness of God (James 1:20). I wish I could say that I never again had a similar outburst, but it was probably another year or two before I learned to bite my tongue when being provoked, and I believe that part of why the Lord began to give me more prophetic words and visions after this season was that I had developed the character to be trusted with more and greater secrets.

Not everything God will show you is intended to be broadcast from the rooftops. There are many things God will show you to inform you, to instruct you, and to have you pray for others or in some other way serve them, but which were never intended to become the subject of dinner conversation or of a targeted sermon.

> Surely the Lord God will do nothing, but he revealeth his secret unto his servants the prophets. (Amos 3:7)

Some things are **supposed** to be a **secret**! There will be times when God will command you to speak, and there are times to remain silent. God may very well have revealed something to you, but it does not always mean that it is to be disclosed. For example, the apostle John heard the voice of the seven thunders during the vision which later became the Book of Revelation, but he was instructed not to write what was said (John 10:4).

Now, don't get me wrong. One thing I also learned during that season was that leaders will often try to cover up things at ought to be exposed because of what that exposure would cost them, and that they will often try to constrain others to silence in the name of discretion. This is a grievous sin on their part, and one they will have to answer to God for. If you have detected sin in the camp that can defile others, seek God's specific direction as to what course to take. Sometimes God may have you pray, and in other scenarios he may very well have you call that sin out in front of the whole church:

> Let the elders that rule well be counted worthy of double honour, especially they who labour in the word and doctrine.
> For the scripture saith, Thou shalt not muzzle the ox that treadeth out the corn. And, The labourer *is* worthy of his reward.
> Against an elder receive not an accusation, but before two or three witnesses.
> Them that sin rebuke before all, that others also may fear.
> I charge *thee* before God, and the Lord Jesus Christ, and the elect angels, that thou observe these things without preferring one before another, doing nothing by partiality. (1 Timothy 5:17-21)

It is clear that in this passage the apostle is instructing

Timothy in the matter of dealing with elders, that is, with **leaders**. He admonishes Timothy to count those who rule well as being worthy of double honor, that they are to be provided for accordingly, that an accusation ought not to be received except with witnesses, and when elders sin, they are to be rebuked openly, so that others will rightly be afraid to sin also. This goes against the grain of contemporary ministry, which tends to try to shield leaders from genuine accountability, and often marginalizes or vilifies those who might call a leader to task for sinful conduct. In the end, you are best served by being certain that, no matter what action you take, that you have clearly heard from God first.

We can also surmise that the prophet who is easily offended is going to have a hard time exercising discipline and discretion, and this tendency can cripple a ministry or even destroy it. It's also a strong indicator that there are very serious defects of character, temperament and integrity yet to be dealt with. I've seen this in action, and it's not pretty. One prophet I knew years ago had a habit of teasing and even ridiculing people, but at the same time couldn't take a joke, and he was **VERY** easily offended. This was particularly true if someone were to say something that pricked his conscience.

Those of us who are easily offended usually do not see themselves as such. Some live in a knowing denial of their oversensitivity, and others have thoroughly convinced themselves that the offenses they experience are indeed worthy of their reaction, or overreaction as the case may be. It may therefore be of significant value to consult with a leader of mature experience and balanced temperament on this matter so that this unfortunate disposition can be corrected.

Whatever our disposition might be, it is best to refrain from being reactive when offended, annoyed, angered, and so on. Always remember that while we were created to have emotions, it was never intended for our emotions to have us. There may even be times when we have good reason to be offended, yet that offense is never to be the motive behind our conduct. Scripture tells us that those who are led by the Spirit of God are the sons of God (Rom. 8:14). For those of us called to the prophetic ministry (and any other ministry) we must always bear in mind that our words and conduct not only have spiritual power, but they also have influence, and therefore they are never without consequence.

Then came the children of Israel, *even* the whole congregation, into the desert of Zin in the first month: and the people abode in Kadesh; and Miriam died there, and was buried there.

And there was no water for the congregation: and they gathered themselves together against Moses and against Aaron. And the people chode with Moses, and spake, saying, Would God that we had died when our brethren died before the Lord! And why have ye brought up the congregation of the Lord into this wilderness, that we and our cattle should die there? And wherefore have ye made us to come up out of Egypt, to bring us in unto this evil place? it *is* no place of seed, or of figs, or of vines, or of pomegranates; neither *is* there any water to drink. And Moses and Aaron went from the presence of the assembly unto the door of the tabernacle of the congregation, and they fell upon their faces: and the glory of the Lord appeared unto them.

And the Lord spake unto Moses, saying, Take the rod, and gather thou the assembly together, thou, and Aaron thy brother, and speak ye unto the rock before their eyes; and it shall give forth his water, and thou shalt bring forth to them water out of the rock: so thou shalt give the congregation and their beasts drink. And Moses took the rod from before the Lord, as he commanded him. And Moses and Aaron gathered the congregation together before the rock, and he said unto them, Hear now, ye rebels; must we fetch you water out of this rock? And Moses lifted up his hand, and with his rod he smote the rock twice: and the water came out abundantly, and the congregation drank, and their beasts *also*. And the Lord spake unto Moses and Aaron, Because ye believed me not, to sanctify me in the eyes of the children of Israel, therefore ye shall not bring this congregation into the land which I have given them. (Numbers 20:1-12)

At this point in their ministry, Moses and Aaron had good reason to be annoyed with God's people. They had complained and murmured just about the whole way from Egypt, despite God having protected and provided for them in a spectacular fashion again and again. However, Moses and Aaron had misrepresented God with their conduct. As a result, Moses was not allowed to bring the children of Israel into the Promised Land, and Aaron had to **die** for his part in the fiasco (v.25-20).

This may at first seem to be a harsh punishment. Yet me must consider that because of the place of leadership Moses and Aaron served in, their conduct could very well have been interpreted to have been indicative of God's disposition toward his people. Likewise, those of us who minister in the prophetic must take care that we conduct ourselves wisely, or we might just be responsible for someone forming an erroneous perception of God and His heart for His people. In today's world of ministry there have been more than a few leaders whose lack of discretion has kept them out of their own promised land, so to speak. This is not just limited to morality, ethics, behavior or attitude, which we will deal with in more detail in Chapter 6. Very often our lapses of discretion occur in the administration of the prophetic gift itself.

As I've said earlier, not everything God shows you is meant to be publicly declared. By the same token, when God has revealed something to you which **is meant** to be disclosed, whether openly or just to certain individuals, it is a dangerous thing to keep it to yourself. One good example would be Jonah, who didn't just try to keep it quiet, he actually got on a ship and tried to leave the region (Jonah 1:3). Jonah's rebellion endangered everyone on that ship, and much in the same way we can prove to be a danger to those around us when we refuse to speak or otherwise disclose something when God has directed us to do so.

The same can be said for personal matters. It is rarely wise to share your more personal feelings, situations, problems with people who don't know you or care about you. Be ready to be led by the spirit in regard to this, since sometimes (rarely) God may have you open up to someone you don't know well just yet. In most cases, though, it is best to reserve your confidence for those who demonstrate maturity, wisdom and love for **you**. People who don't care for you are more likely to take something spoken in confidence and attempt to use it to slander you. Yes, they will be wrong to do so, but at the end of the day it will have been you who made the unwise choice to disclose information to them that might well have been better kept in the close confidence of those who could be trusted with it. Such indiscretion can be detrimental not just to you, but to those to whom you might have ministered to, but who may not be disposed to receiving anything from you because of what they have heard, true or not. There may very well be times when you are slandered for no cause, but the truth of the matter is that it's best to not to create opportunities for such things. God **can** cause rumors, slanders, and even a true report of fault or wrong on your part to be of no effect, but it often occurs that we do have to live with the consequences of things said and done unwisely.

Yet for some prophets the greatest danger to the faithful execution of their ministry is not a willful refusal to prophesy because they, like Jonah want to see someone "get it." In many cases, it's not even the tendency to disclose God's revelations in anger, or for selfish reasons. For some prophets I've known over the years, the most grave threat to their ministry is carelessness. There are some prophets out there who may not be eager to spill the beans on everything they hear or see prophetically, but who are instead lacking in the self-control necessary to keep them from letting the proverbial cat out of the bag.

I have spent most of my life around prophets and those with the gift of prophecy, and I have over time observed that a great number of them ceased to hear from God regularly, and quite a few stopped hearing from God at all. In some cases it was because of a lukewarmness in their relationship with God, or outright backsliding, but in cases in which they still appeared to have a zeal from God and were not in any obvious sin, the culprit was carelessness. Many of them were quite capable of turning a prophetic message into the subject of gossip, or would let something slip that God had entrusted them to keep in confidence. Still others made errors of presumption in how they handled what God had said through them or others. In any case, heart of the problem is in fact a lack of reverence.

> And they set the ark of God upon a new cart, and brought it out of the house of Abinadab that *was* in Gibeah: and Uzzah and Ahio, the sons of Abinadab, drave the new cart.
> And they brought it out of the house of Abinadab which *was* at Gibeah, accompanying the ark of God: and Ahio went before the ark.
> And David and all the house of Israel played before the Lord on all manner of *instruments made of* fir wood, even on harps, and on psalteries, and on timbrels, and on cornets, and on cymbals.
> And when they came to Nachon's threshingfloor, Uzzah put forth *his hand* to the ark of God, and took hold of it; for the oxen shook *it.*
> And the anger of the Lord was kindled against Uzzah; and God smote him there for *his* error; and there he died by the ark of God. (II Samuel 6:3-7)

At first, God's punishment of Uzzah may seem harsh. However, God had given Israel very specific instructions as to how the Ark should be handled and transported, which was on specially made poles to be handled **only** by the Kohathites. The mere fact of transporting it by cart was bad enough, but for Uzzah to even be involved in its transport was disrespectful to God, since he was not a Kohathite, but just one of the sons of the man whose house the Ark had been in. Had it been transported with its poles on the shoulders of the Kohathites, the Ark would not have tipped, and there would have been no need for Uzzah to be within arm's length of it.

We must always be diligent in how we handle the things of God. When we treat any aspect of our service to God carelessly, we insult him. Some of you will perhaps say that God isn't running around killing people for insulting him these days, that we're in the New Testament, we're under 'grace,' and so on.

Perhaps its best that we remember than Annanias and Sapphira were also under 'grace.' (Acts 5). Now, considering that, think for a moment of how disposed you are to carry on a conversation with someone who keeps insulting you. While God is not a man, and while he is above our human tendency to be easily offended, he is GOD. Shall we not treat what he has placed in our hands with dignity, reverence, and diligence? In any case, our motive in being discreet in how we handle anything God has entrusted to us ought not to be a fear of punishment, but rather a loving desire to do what is pleasing to the Lord, and to carry out our respective assignments with love, honor, integrity and wisdom. Remember, the more trustworthy you are, the more you will be trusted with, both in the prophetic and in life in general.

A Prayer for discretion:

Father, please forgive me for every time I have acted unwisely, carelessly, or pridefully, both in everyday life and in the things you have committed to my care. Grant me a wise and understanding heart that I might conduct myself wisely and bring honor to your name in all that I do, in Jesus' name.

Putting it into action:

1. Get a small notebook and pen and keep them handy. Begin keeping track of when you speak or act unwisely, carelessly, etc. This is not for the purpose of condemnation, or of trying to better yourself through your own strength. It will, however, give you a better understanding of the circumstances, influences, and ideas connected with your own tendency toward indiscretion, be it great or small.

2. Weigh your words more carefully. The Bible tells us that those who are wise consider their answer before they speak (Proverbs 15:28). Begin to make a habit of waiting before you speak, and practice being less ready to give your opinion on everything.

3. Take time to study those who are noteworthy for their wisdom, and engage them if you can. Wise people are often very willing to share what they have learned, so you will do well to

surround yourself with as many of them as you can.

4. Invest in relationships with people who will hold you accountable. It's very easy to become blind to one's own defects and faults, but as the Bible tells us, there is safety in the multitude of counselors (Proverbs 15:22)

KEY #5: INTEGRITY

Now if you walk before Me as your father David walked, in integrity of heart and in uprightness, to do according to all that I have commanded you, *and* if you keep My statutes and My judgments, then I will establish the throne of your kingdom over Israel forever, as I promised David your father, saying, 'You shall not fail to have a man on the throne of Israel. (1 Kings 9:4-5)

Although David had some problems, most notably in regard to the matter of Uriah the Hittite (2 Samuel 11). However, aside from that very notable and consequently destructive misconduct, David had walked in integrity. For the purpose of this writing, it is this we shall focus on. However, before we delve into the matter of personal and ministerial integrity, let us more carefully examine the above passage.

God makes a promise to Solomon, and one of particular interest to a king. Every king in his right mind wants his dominion to last, and he wants it to continue in its present strength or greater long after he has died. God tells Solomon that if he walks in integrity, obeying everything that God has commanded him to do, and keeping his Law, then he will always have a man on Israel's throne. Now, you may be thinking that we are not the kings of Israel, nor of any other earthly realm, and while that is certainly true, and while no prophecy of scripture is of any private interpretation (2 Peter 1:20), God's statements in the Bible do serve to reveal his nature to us.

That having been said, if we understand that spiritually speaking, God has made us kings and priests (e.g., 1 Peter:2:9; Revelation 1:5-6), then there is a degree of authority, power, and majesty which has has ordained for each of us. These may be overt and obvious, or they may very well be quiet and unobtrusive, but they are intended for us nonetheless. We should also consider that God's promise for the continuity of Solomon's kingdom reveals another aspect of his intention for us, whether we walk in the prophetic or not: the impact and influence of the authority God has purposed for us is also intended to extend beyond us, and even beyond our lifetimes. There may be aspects of your vision that God has intended to be started by you, but completed by others, whether by those of future generations physically, or by your spiritual offspring. It is also of the utmost importance that we keep in mind that fathers tend to acquire most of their honor through their sons. Abraham was given the Promise, but it was in Isaac that his seed was blessed, and it was Jacob who sired the patriarchs of the nation that bore his new name, Israel. And yet, even these did not receive the fulness of the promise. Their descendant, Moses, brought Israel to the Promised Land, but his successor brought them **in**, while it was David who finally conquered it, and the ultimate manifestation of the great Promise of Abraham came by way of Jesus Christ. We would do well to remember, that the name of Jesus has been exalted above every name **for the glory of God the Father** (Philippians 2:9-11). Thus, we must remember that integrity is not only the key to the manifestation of the kings God called us to be, but it is also crucial to the rise of those sons whose work will bring God's honor upon the work which the Lord first committed to us.

Integrity is more than just avoiding the various pitfalls of obvious sin, though it is difficult to overstate the need for a holy life. Some of us are good at avoiding the more flagrant kinds of sin, but still allow room for seemingly minor (and yet often no less problematic) lapses of conduct, conscience and composure to occur. In King Solomon's case, the slide into flagrant disobedience began immediately after he used deception to take revenge on Shimei in 1 Kings 2. David had promised not to kill Shimei for cursing him years before, and he instructed Solomon:

And, behold, you *hast* with you Shimei the son of Gera, a Benjamite of Bahurim, which cursed me with a grievous curse in the day when I went to Mahanaim: but he came down to meet me at Jordan, and I sware to him by the Lord, saying, I will not put you to death with the sword.

Now therefore hold him not guiltless: for thou *art* a wise man, and you know what thou ought to do unto him; but his grey head bring down to the grave with blood. (1 Kings 2:8-9)

It was immediately after the events of this chapter that Solomon marries Pharaoh's daughter in direct disobedience to God's command to never marry **ANY** foreign woman. He then goes on to take many foreign wives and concubines, and later we are told that this was the cause of his downfall (1 Samuel 11:1-13).

What can we learn from Solomon? Deception of any kind is to be shunned. Solomon renewed David's promise of amnesty, but with an added condition which he **knew** Shimei would not be able to abide by. Now, some people in prophetic ministry will actually use this as an example of wisdom, and invariably these prophets turn out to be people who will deliberately lay spiritual traps for others. The oversensitive prophet I mentioned earlier was one. He would say or do something which he knew would get under someone's skin, and then use any negative reaction on their part as 'proof' that they were in rebellion or had some manner of demonic bondage. This, of course, wasn't wisdom. In some cases it may have been effective in exposing people who were rebellious, but in most cases it only served to annoy, anger, or humiliate people who already had problems and didn't need a prophet setting them up for a public scolding that had no clear purpose other than aggrandizement of the leader. It's not constructive. There may be times when you'll have to openly rebuke people, but do so only by the direction of the Holy Spirit, or you may very well alienate people sent by God to help you in your mission.

We can always argue that people should take it better, or that they shouldn't let those things get to them, but it is unwise in any leadership capacity to expect people to behave as they should. Rather, we should expect that people are going to be people:

flawed, moody, sullen, scared, hurting, and so on. In any form of ministry, relying on your own opinion in administering your gift is a direct contravention of God's command:

> Trust in the Lord with all your heart, and lean not on your own understanding. In all your ways acknowledge him, and he will direct your path. (Proverbs 3:5-6)

This simple admonition will keep you from making easy but costly mistakes that will violate the integrity of your priesthood. Heed it well.

I once encountered a young prophetess who, while gifted, had some serious issues of integrity. She quickly boasted to me that she had several churches, and invited me to one of her services. I finally came to one, which turned out to be a weekly meeting in a seniors/disabled facility. At first this seemed like a lovely idea, establishing a church in this small community of people who often had limited mobility and means of transportation. Then I noticed that one of the senior citizens was sitting at the security desk.

To make a long story short, this prophetess worked at the building as a security guard, and had one of the residents covering her post while she conducted the church service **during work hours**. Had her employer found out, she would have been fired, and rightly so. Consider that while she was being 'spiritual' and 'prophetic,' she was exposing her employer to tremendous liability in the event that a serious breach of security occurred while she was away from her post. As I got to know her a bit more, I soon learned that this was not the only major integrity gap in her life. Not surprisingly her 'prophecies' were often incomplete, disjointed, and even completely wrong. Now, some prophets can continue to be accurate while engaging in rotten behavior. However, that is often more an indicator of God's grace toward the people being ministered to than toward the prophet, and the prophet in question may soon find himself on the wrong side of God's corrective judgment.

Never mistake God's forbearance for his approval.

Too many prophets have a tendency to 'change' gears in their personality and are often a totally different person in the pulpit than they are behind the scenes. Even when there's no obvious sin involved, this is often an indicator that there's problem with one's integrity. Why? Putting on a different demeanor or mannerisms for the purposes of a pulpit performance is dishonest, and it points to a desire for self-aggrandizement. It's one thing to strive for excellence in how you present yourself and your message, and in how you represent God, but it's another thing entirely to put up an act that misrepresents who you really are. Christ was the same man whether teaching the multitudes or attending the funeral of his good friend Lazarus. Is the servant greater than his master? (John 15:20)

A Prayer over one's integrity:

Father, forgive me for any way in which I have lacked integrity, and help me to become more like your Son in my behavior, attitude, and character. Deliver me from all pride, selfishness and wrong thinking that would cause me to err, and let me be whole in every way, in Jesus' name.

Putting it into action:

1. Pay closer attention to your integrity. When you have had a lapse, great or small, don't just get it right with God in terms of forgiveness, write it down and examine yourself to see what habits and tendencies led to any such lapse, so that you can more decisively deal with the root causes of these problems and not just the symptoms. Yes, God can convict you, but he also commands us to examine ourselves (1 Corinthians 11:28, e.g.)

2. Enlist the aid of several spiritually mature people who genuinely love you to hold you accountable. These should be people you trust, and with whom you can be transparent.

38

KEY #6: BE USEFUL

Surely the Lord God will do nothing without revealing His secret to His servants the prophets. (Amos 3:7)

Usually in the prophetic ministry we tend to think of this scripture solely in terms of God revealing privileged information exclusively to the prophets, and all too often it becomes a source of misplaced pride and conceit. While it is indeed a great privilege to be on the receiving end of God's secrets, there is yet a greater meaning within this scripture that unlocks a whole new depth of prophetic revelation and understanding.

What is this great key? He reveals his secrets to his SERVANTS the prophets. Now, this doesn't imply that all prophets are good servants. It is, however, a call to be useful and profitable servants.

Let's face it. Many of us in the prophetic ministry have a great desire to be used in prophecy, but at the same time we'll disregard numerous opportunities to serve God and his purposes in other ways. Usually, we'll make some excuse which will be made to sound spiritual, like "I don't feel that's what God's called me to," or 'I'm really not gifted in that area." Now, while we shouldn't try to be something we aren't, and we would do well to abide in our respective calling (1 Corinthians 7:24), usually really we're just trying to avoid doing something we consider inconvenient, unglamorous, or just plain tiresome.

Not everything that God wants us to do is going to be outwardly great, grandiose, or even obvious ministry, and there are times that we should seek to make ourselves useful in things that aren't necessarily part of our overall purpose. How do we know this?

39

But who is there of you, having a servant plowing or keeping sheep, that will say unto him, when he is come in from the field, Come straightway and sit down to meat;
and will not rather say unto him, Make ready wherewith I may sup, and gird thyself, and serve me, till I have eaten and drunken; and afterward thou shalt eat and drink?
Doth he thank the servant because he did the things that were commanded?

> Even so ye also, when ye shall have done all the things that are commanded you, say, We are unprofitable servants; we have done that which it was our duty to do. (Luke 17:7-10)

If we've only done our duty, we have surely missed out on opportunities to be of further service to God and his kingdom. Usually these aren't big things, but they are often small things which, while not required of us, can accelerate our growth and lend a greater depth to our experiences. This, in turn, enriches the calibre and gravity of our message within our purpose.

When I lived in Trenton, NJ, I attended a small church led by a prophet, and after reading *Spiritual Authority* by Watchman Nee, I was eager to avail myself of the spiritual riches to be had from submission to authority. One of the things I had gleaned from my reading of that book was that genuine submission to authority led to an inevitable transfer of the anointing of the authority figure onto the individual who was submitting. Since I had (and still have) an earnest desire to grow spiritually, I made it my mission to try to make myself useful.

So, I joined the worship ministry. I wasn't a great singer, but the worship leader did like my voice, and I was faithful in trying to be helpful to her efforts. I also became the nearly-ever-present helper of the deacons, the de-factor church janitor, and even joined the newly formed dance ministry to try encourage its leader. I didn't stop there, because by now being useful had become a bit of a habit.

This habit carried over into my daily life, and I sought

opportunities to represent God well everywhere I went. I'm sure I raised eyebrows around town when people would see me sitting at a bus stop just shooting the breeze with a drug addict or a prostitute, but I felt it was a good thing to interact with them whenever I had time to do so. It wasn't always about preaching to them, but often it was rather just about being kind and friendly, because I knew that for many of them it wasn't too often that 'normal' people treated them like human beings, like they mattered. I would also help people with personal errands, projects, home repairs, and other things because I knew that God's presence in my life would not be idle while I interacted with them and did things with and for them. Now, we may not all have the energy to be that active, and that's okay. The important thing is simply to keep our eyes open for ways we can be useful to the kingdom without compromising our own purpose.

Being useful often produces other outcomes as well. In the epistle to Philemon, Paul writes of the escaped slave, Onesimus: I appeal to you for my child, Onesimus, whose father I became in my imprisonment. (Formerly he was useless to you, but now he is indeed useful to you and to me.) I am sending him back to you, sending my very heart. I would have been glad to keep him with me, in order that he might serve me on your behalf during my imprisonment for the gospel, but I preferred to do nothing without your consent in order that your goodness might not be by compulsion but of your own accord. For this is perhaps why he was parted from you for a while, that you might have him back forever, no longer as a slave, as a beloved brother—especially to me, but how much more to you, both in the flesh and in the Lord. (Philemon 1:10-16)

It is reported in some accounts that this was the same Onesimus who went on to become the Bishop of Ephesus. Some authorities doubt this, but in any case, we can see here that at the very least, Onesimus was released from the bondage of slavery because he had been useful. Likewise, for many saints, there are kinds of bondage that are often connected to or even caused by idleness, both spiritual and natural. If this seems to be a strange idea, consider the fact that the bondage of obesity is readily broken by exercise and activity. The bondage of ignorance can be destroyed through learning, and so on. It also often happens that a great part of why people are unable to move on from hurtful events is that they commit too much time to dwelling on those events instead of finding something useful to do in the present. There is a great deal of truth in the old adage that idle hands are the devil's workshop.

A Prayer to be useful:

Father, forgive for every time I was able to be of use to your cause and others, but I did not take action because of idleness, selfishness, or any other reason. I thank you for helping me to see more clearly how I can make myself available to be a help to those around me, in Jesus name.

Putting it into action:

1. Take some time to reflect on the people around you. Consider ways in which your skills, personal qualities, and influence can be helpful. Remember, this is **not** about **you.** Look for those small opportunities to serve that may arise here and there, and make yourself useful.

2. Devote at least some of your prayer time to seeking God about how you might best be useful even beyond the scope and scale of your own calling.

KEY #7: LOVE

A new commandment I give unto you, That ye love one another; as I have loved you, that ye also love one another. By this shall all men know that ye are my disciples, if ye have love one to another.
--John 13:34-35

Love, much like forgiveness, is a decision. Christ himself said that everyone would know that we were his disciples if we have love for one another. Why is this? We live in a world in which selfishness does not simply abound; it is often praised. In the business world, there is a saying, 'Greed is good.' If we are to be truly distinct from the world, we in the prophetic ministry (and otherwise) must operate in genuine godly love.

Now, love isn't just about good feelings. When Christ prayed that fateful night in the garden of Gethsemane, he declared that God loved his disciples as he had loved Jesus. Now, bear in mind that God had not only allowed Christ's suffering, but had actually orchestrated it. Jesus Christ, the author and finisher of our faith, was no less loving when he took the time to braid a whip and then drove corrupt businessmen out of the temple (John 2:14-16).

If we are to truly minister in love, then we must act in the best interests of those to whom we minister, as defined by the Word of God. Now, in the prophetic ministry it often occurs that people tend to be very committed to 'tough love,' even when it isn't really appropriate. Some will use the above example of Christ moving in correction to justify strong-arm tactics and to validate ruling over God's people with an iron hand. However, we have to understand that Christ's actions in the temple were in the interest of restoring the sanctity of God's house, and of protecting God's people from the predations of wily salespeople. The prophetic minister (or anyone else) who operates in real love is going to be tough only

43

when it's necessary, and will pursue a commitment to the patterns and paradigms of Biblical truth.

Another essential truth about love is that is causes people to listen, in two different ways. First, if we are motivated by love we will be more at to listen to what people are saying (and what the are not saying), and our ministering will be all the better for it. Yes, some prophetic ministers will make the claim that they 'just listen to God,' but the truth of the matter is that such assertions are usually grounded in arrogance and laziness. It's arrogance because they are often presuming that they are hearing clearly from God with respect to absolutely everything (doubtful at best), and laziness because very often they just aren't interested in taking the trouble to hear people out. There may be times when God will lead you to disregard what people are saying, but there are also times when God will **not** clue you in on everything that's going on because he intends for you to listen. Always keep this in mind: there will be many times when someone you are ministering to has something useful to say, and even something which God intended to be of benefit to **you**, or others. When you genuinely love people, you will care enough to listen to them. Sometimes the prophetic answer they need may come out of their own mouth as they pour their heart out.

The other way that love can cause people to listen is in the sense that our genuine love can make people more receptive to what we have to say. Years ago there was a brother in the church who was by most counts considered to be a 'problem' saint. Frequent backsliding and stubbornness were among his more salient character traits. He just wouldn't listen to anyone. Not surprisingly, he was regarded as a rebel and treated as such because of his apparent resistance to authority figures. His own pastor seemed to believe that the cure for this tendency was public humiliation, and of course it backfired.

While rebellion was definitely one of his problems, it wasn't the root cause of it all. The true underlying issue was rejection, largely with respect to his relationship with his father. So the harsh methods of leadership absent of genuine love and the tendency of such leadership to come down hard on anyone who seemed rebellious in any way could **never** be productive with this man. Much to the surprise of the other men around, this particular brother would not only listen to me, but would obey whatever instructions I gave him without question. We had all belonged to a group of men which would meet six days a week for early morning prayer, so we'd spent a fair amount of time around each other. One day. he told the men in the group, "I listen to Brother Sam because I know Brother Sam loves me." Despite the fact that I had at times rebuked him as sternly as anyone else had, he always knew that I had his best interest at heart and genuinely cared about him.

Never underestimate the power of genuine, godly love to cause people to take heed to what God is saying through you, and always be mindful that a lack of love on our part can easily cause people to reject our message. Yes, some people will claim you are 'unloving' just for telling them the truth, but if you are honest with yourself about your motives and conduct, you will know better than to fall prey to such childish manipulation.

Love will temper your motives. It happens much too often in the prophetic ministry that prophets will use their gift to entice people into serving the exclusive self interest of the prophet. I knew of one church where the prophetess has her church members cleaning her house, washing her car, doing her laundry, and more. While it is good for us to serve one another, it's a wicked thing to use one's place of authority to manipulate people into becoming one's one personal entourage of flunkies.

Other prophets will use prophecy as a means of enticing people to give larger gifts of money. Watch videos of popular prophets in action, and some patterns will quickly emerge. One is to connect prophecy with offerings of money, for the obvious purpose of manipulating people into giving more than they normally would in the hope of getting a better prophecy. Another pattern is the tendency of the prophet to make sure he finds the gift satisfactory before he prophesies. Some do this efficiently by having a $500 line, a $100 line, a $50 line, and so on. The people in the $500 line get grand and lofty 'prophecies,' whereas if you're in the $10 line, you may not be prophesied to at all. Other prophets will simply look at the offering in the person's hand first. With one very popular prophet, this is a very consistent habit. If the person approaches with a check, he will stand there and read the check first, and when he doesn't like the amount, it's clear from his facial expression and he hurries the individual along with a vague and sometimes obviously contrived 'prophecy.'

Do such practices reflect a genuine love of God? I think not. Some in the world of prophetic ministry will point to a few scriptural examples where someone brought a gift to a prophet as justification for such chicanery, but the truth is that most Biblical prophets tended to refuse gifts, and very often the gifts they did receive were a token only, and not of considerable monetary value. One of the most popular examples is that story in 1 Samuel 9:

> And when they were come to the land of Zuph, Saul said to his servant that was with him, Come, and let us return; lest my father leave caring for the asses, and take thought for us.
> And he said unto him, Behold now, there is in this city a man of God, and he is an honourable man; all that he saith cometh surely to pass: now let us go thither; peradventure he can shew us our way that we should go.
> Then said Saul to his servant, But, behold, if we go, what shall we bring the man? for the bread is spent in our vessels, and there is not a present to bring to the man of God: what have we?
> And the servant answered Saul again, and said, Behold, I have here at hand the fourth part of a shekel of silver: that will I give to the man of God, to tell us our way. (1 Samuel 9:5-8)

A shekel is approximately 10.5 grams. At the time of this writing, silver was approximately $1 per gram. So, the amount of money Saul's servant proposed to give to the man of God was a little more than $2.50, hardly a princely sum, and yet this is the scripture often

46

used to justify the flagrant fleecing of God's people for a prophecy.

Perhaps some in the prophetic ministry would still insist that they are doing nothing wrong by demanding money for prophecy, or giving the impression that giving a 'better' offering will result in a 'better' prophecy. In my conversations with numerous prophets over the years on this matter, the most common objection raised to the truth behind the account of 1 Samuel 9 is usually expressed in terms of self-interest and how they have a 'right' to be 'blessed' by their ministering.

> Though I speak with the tongues of men and of angels, but have not love, I have become sounding brass or a clanging cymbal. And though I have *the gift of* prophecy, and understand all mysteries and all knowledge, and though I have all faith, so that I could remove mountains, but have not love, I am nothing. And though I bestow all my goods to feed *the poor*, and though I give my body to be burned, but have not love, it profits me nothing.
> Love suffers long *and* is kind; love does not envy; love does not parade itself, is not puffed up; does not behave rudely, DOES NOT SEEK ITS OWN, is not provoked, thinks no evil; does not rejoice in iniquity, but rejoices in the truth; bears all things, believes all things, hopes all things, endures all things. (1 Cotinthians 13:1-7, emhpasis mine)

Now, I know someone will bring up Paul's assertion that those who preach the gospel ought to live from the gospel (1 Corinthians 9:14). This is certainly true, but Paul at the same time did whatever was in his power to keep from being a burden to the church, because he did not want to put any obstacle in the way of the gospel. While we who serve as leaders in the body of Christ have a right to live from our labor, we never have a right to give people the impression that access to the gifts of God is a privilege based on what dollar amount they are giving. Freely we have received, freely we must give (Matthew 10:8), and freely we ought to trust God to provide for us rather than attempt to goad people into giving in exchange for prophecy, especially given that God declared his judgment against those who do so in Micah 3:11. Therein, my brethren is the heart of the matter. Never use what you think are your rights to pursue your self-interest. While many of today's Christian leaders will say self-interest is a not bad thing, we must bear in mind what Paul wrote:

> I am crucified with Christ, nevertheless I live, yet not I, but Christ lives in me, and the life that I now live in the flesh i live by the faith of the Son of God, who loved me and gave himself for me. (Galatians 2:20)

If then we are crucified with Christ, and we live by his faith, then an exclusive self-interest has no place in our life. If we live for Christ, then even whatever we do for our financial well-being, for the care of our bodies, for our families, and so on should be really done in the interest of the cause of Christ, and in keeping with his ways. Thus, one of the easiest ways to know whether we are acting in love is by taking an honest look at our true motives. If we're being selfish, love has definitely taken a backseat at best.

A Prayer for a renewed commitment to godly love:

Father, forgive me for falling short in exercising love to those around me. Fill me with a genuine love for you and for others, so that my motives will be clean and my purpose pure. Cleanse me of all bitterness, resentment, hatred, malice, envy and every other unclean work that might yet be within me, and let my life be characterized by your love, in Jesus' name.

Putting it into action:

1. Love is a decision, so decide today to exercise it well.
2. Make a list of people you don't like, and another list of people who have done you wrong. Now, pray for them daily.
3. For one week, keep track of your motives in the things that you do. Write them down if you can, and at the end of the week, see where you need to make some changes.

CONCLUSION

A call to the prophetic ministry is a beautiful and delicate privilege. As such, we ought to handle the prophetic with care, diligence, and dignity. It is likely that we may make some mistakes along the way, commit some errors, and perhaps even have some lapses of good judgment and integrity, but it doesn't have to be that way. As the Bible says, God is well able to keep us from falling (Jude 1:24).

Thus, we can make a choice to pursue these seven key principles in our journey toward maturity in the prophetic. They are not difficult to follow, but they are also easy not to bother with. Ultimately, we will each have to decide for ourselves whether we truly believe that the purpose of God for our lives is worth it. It is my prayer that everyone who reads this little book will be blessed by it, and encouraged to pursue a closer walk with God that will bring them to maturity not only in their gifts, but in their purpose.

God bless you, and God keep you.

ABOUT THE AUTHOR

Sam Medina is an award winning artist and writer as well as the Chairman of The Restoration Group, an apostolic ministry committed to the equipping and releasing of uncompromising Christians and Christian leaders in every walk of life, and to building strong communities of believers who will be living epistles of the Gospel, edifying, encouraging, and supporting one another in their respective callings.

A dynamic teacher of the word, Sam has spoken at churches, community organizations, and business events throughout North America, and oversees a growing network of international ministries dedicated to the spread of the Gospel throughout the world.

You can connect with him online:
http://www.restorationgroup.org
http://www.twitter.com/Kingdom_Apostle
http://www.sam-medina.com

Printed in Great Britain
by Amazon